# MELTING

*Poems of a Frozen Man*

To Eric,

we touch the
~~same soul~~,

מ'י'ג'נו

*[signature]*

# Melting

## POEMS OF A FROZEN MAN

*Jerry Steinberg*

ECW PRESS

CANADIAN CATALOGUING IN PUBLICATION DATA

Steinberg, Jerry

Melting : poems of a frozen man

ISBN 1-55022-174-4
I. Title.

PS8587.T45M4 1992   C811'.54   C92-095252-6
PR9199.3.S84M4 1992

Published with the financial assistance of
The Canada Council and the Ontario Arts Council

The cover features a glass sculpture by Carol-Ann Casselman,
from the artist's "Cassel-Ice" series. Photograph by Thomas Moore.
Photograph of the author by Dahlia Steinberg.
Set in Monotype Poliphilus & Blado by ECW Type & Art, Oakville, Ontario
Printed and bound by The Porcupine's Quill, Inc., Erin, Ontario

Distributed by General Publishing Co. Limited
30 Lesmill Road, Don Mills, Ontario M3B 2T6

Published by ECW PRESS,
1980 Queen Street East, Second Floor,
Toronto, Ontario M4L 1J2

*to my father*
       *who sings and hums*
                *in death's shadow*

# Woman-Floe

They say I'm not frozen.

                all these women

     How do they know

    Taken in by my smile

                     warm they say

          by my eyes

                    kind they say

          by my voice

                    gentle they say

          by my touch

                    soft they say

       what do they know

         of the icicles in my veins

                that scratch my heart

         of the frost in my blood

                that bites my breath

         of the chill in my core

                that cuts my soul

   what do they know

         what do they know

You stood
    with your back to the balcony
        on the second floor
   suddenly
      you were sucked away from me
      back
        back
      through the door
        over the railing
          to the cement below
   I ran
     ice gripping my heart
     and saw you lying there
         still
     and I shouted
        screamed
     I've lost her
     I've lost her
  and awoke
     trembling
       sweating
   awakening you
     telling you my nightmare
and somewhere inside
      you shuddered
   because you knew it was true
while I calmed down
      whispering
  thank⁄God
   it's only a dream

You said
       don't touch me
            not ever again
        I can't stand your touch
    and with that
           we ended our marriage
        I retreated into myself
          doubting
               any woman
      would ever want me to touch her
          doubting
                I could ever be loved
                  or give love again
          doubting
                the degree to which I was human
        suspecting
              deep inside
        I was somehow diseased
        and before long
              would expire

There's been a clearing
       after our talk
          old friend
               and once wife
   something has shifted
          in my chest
    and there's a feeling of lightness
             about me
     like a healing has taken place
     a healthy distancing
          from the one I love
    and a special coming together
      with you
           after many years

You looked at me
     and said simply
          you have beautiful eyes
no woman
     had ever said that to me
          before
    I stared at you
       in disbelief
      surely you must be joking
         but you weren't
I was almost dead
     when you said those words
   parched and dried up
     not touched
       or loved
        for years
you let me drink from your well
    enough
      for new stirrings
        in my loins
         in my heart
          in my soul
  enough
    to bring blossoms
       into my desert

You held my head on your breast
                           that night
          when I came home
                   full of pain in my chest
          not knowing
                   a year of not being touched
                           had taken such a toll
          not knowing
                           my heart was shrinking
                           my chest turning inward
          you just held me
                   and all that pain
                           all that hidden anguish
                                   drained away
          I knew then
                   I had to be touched
                                   to survive
          I knew then
                   I couldn't live
                           without it

I'm afraid to get too close
                 charcoals in my heart
Afraid to love too much
                 smudges on my soul
Afraid to blend
          and merge
           fences in my breath
Afraid to lose myself
             in your self
       endless caves
      to disappear
             forever
     gone   gone
  and expire
         on your breast

Come close
    It's in my loneliness
        that I need you
Come close
    The spaces inside are cracking
    I feel the icy winds
      as they pass from my seams
And scream into the jagged night

I'm a loving man
       with ugly parts
   wanting you to see
          those parts
    and not shy away
  wanting you to accept
           my ugliness
      even when I can't
 wanting you
      to kiss them
           into swans
     into feathered doves
        of pure whiteness
wanting you to pick them up again
    when they drop into the mud
          these parts
   and with your smile
      tell me
        it's okay
          to be ugly
            sometimes

Tonight I'll let you look
                beneath my skin
        be gentle with me
            for not all the wounds
                        are healed
              not all the bruises
                    soothed

I don't want to save you
                    anymore
        like I have all my life
                woman after woman
        acting to your pain
                masking my own
        the master rescuer

After we parted
        you were desolate
                not because I left
        but because there was no man
                    in your life

This is hard to say
                    because I'm a nice guy
I knew there was a chance
                    that night
            you might call
        and nice guys
                    don't do things like this
When I was making love
                    to another woman
        and I didn't put my answering machine on
                    and you called
        especially nice guys like me
                    with morals and ethics
        and I answered the phone
Part of me
            please remember I'm a nice guy
        hoping it was you
        wanting you to hurt
                    in sweet jealous agony
        wanting you to miss me like crazy
        wanting you to come back to me
                                on one knee
And you did hurt
                while something in me smiled
            nice guys smile a lot

you seedy bastard
   whoever gave you the right
     to spill your juice
       into my woman's womb
    put your cock to better use
         elsewhere
   on some distant
        unseemly flesh⁄cup
   and hold your balls
      in store
     for another market

I don't want to be with a woman
    who doesn't like men
        but doesn't yet know this
    a woman who touches with one hand
            and squeezes with the other
    a woman who kisses
        with needles in her mouth
I don't want to be with a woman
        who hates her father
            but pretends she doesn't
        who wants a man
            because she's lonely
    and who fools herself
                into thinking
        that only with a man
            can she be happy
                and fulfilled
I don't want to be with a woman
        who doesn't understand
            her inner man
    and tries to find him
            everywhere
            but in her soul

We must fight each other
               or love will fail
    slay one another
                  over again
   or death will prevail
There is a cleansing in our combat
     even as we lick our wounds
       a purification
               in our ordeal
       that makes no sense
          but is right
             and feels good
     giving us
          another chance

I want to cock you
        up and down and sideways
            without mercy
                thrust into your womb
                  till my juice
                      runs from your nipples
I want to suck you
        inside out
     bury my tongue
           between your lips
       and die
           amidst your ecstasy
I want to lick you
        every pore
         every hair
           every opening
     and watch you glisten
              in the morning light

Stripes over your breasts
               shadow bars
                   and pale light in⁄between
     I feel you
             sense you
                 touch you from inside
     I know you
             from somewhere
   come
         be with me
             shaded lady
                 soft soul
         come
             we will kiss
                 between the bars

I want to see you
        in the quiet hours
    when sleep
        has taken the masks
    that hide your soul

I want to see you
        in the gentle dawn
    when the soft light
        illumines your face

I want to see you
        amid the dreams
    of future days
    when the sun
        reflects your smile

I love your juice
                filling me up
        bathing my balls
                with wondrous strokes
unparching my cock
                in papered wetness

We stood there in the mountains
and listened to the universe
there was no other sound
I felt in awe
like some mighty spirit
had descended
upon the slopes
enveloping the two of us
in feathered silence
we feared to speak
lest a sin be done
and scarce a breath
passed from our souls

Rub me
    with your nipple
      softly
        in all the places
          you know
            so well
     gently
       over my hair
      exquisite
         the touch of angels
         in heat

When you're sick
       I love you less
    I know I'm not supposed to
         and I do make it up
               by caring more
       but
          you're less whole
            less life
            less fun
      and love needs
             more urging

I remember you telling me
        how you used to hold
                your man's balls
      every night
        falling asleep
           softly cradled
                  in your hand
      your touch
           his lullaby

*thinking my cock touches your soul is bullshit. a conceit. My cock touches my soul when I fuck. the rest is just a delusion.*

When we make love
             my cock touches your soul
             and nudges your heart
       the gods smile and chuckle
                   some even laugh
          at the spaces in us
             that we touch
                         with such delight
We speak our own language
             and they understand
                   even when we don't
       such words and such sounds
          till nothing more is said
          the echoes lying still
          rippling us to sleep

Her feet were exquisite
    I remember the first time I saw them
  like watching a goddess
                  alight upon the earth
      every toe
          every nail
        every vein
              etched into perfection
    her instep
        made me want to stare for hours
            transfixed
     and her ankles
       invited my fingers
         for endless caressing
each foot had a life of its own
       like twins
           in perfect harmony
    beating their own individual rhythm
     on the long mountain grass
I loved her steps
    and remember them still
       softly on my heart

I love you still
            though you move past memories
I love you
            with deep softness
                        feeling you through
                                    forgotten dreams
                                                and drifting hopes
I love you
            in whispered tones
                                                of open silence
I love you
            with a sense of dignity
                        that binds our souls
                                    in a game yet to be played


I love you still

I realized tonight
    that it's easier to be in love
        with fantasy
           than with reality
not that I didn't know this before
    but tonight
        for some reason
    there is a clarity in this
        that wasn't there before
like my head and stomach
        are finally getting together
Both Gabriele and Dona
    I fell in love with
        after they were gone
        after I had lost them
    my heart
        refused to remember
           the reality
    indulging instead
        in an ideal that never was
now
    before me
        lies the onerous task
    of falling in love
        with reality

love is

        between the legs

               my dear

          spread wide

               to the bed⁄posts

   all the rest

               is delusion

My love
    you fill my moments
       and touch me
        as softly
          as the shade
            touches the grass

Last night
    your juices
        were so sweet
     I took honey
        from your comb
      and spread it over
        your skin
          with my tongue
      you glistened
        in the candlelight
      your body
        shimmering
     with each flicker
     your night dew
        whispering love
          and love
          and more love

When we don't
        rub against each other
                in common ways
    we rub against each other
                in strange ways
                    uncomfortable ways
                    pot⁄hole ways
                  washboard ways
   until
        we rub against each other
            again
                in common ways

Death
is on your mind
in your soul
across your face
it keeps coming out
in the water
in the air
in my arms
I hold you
and kiss your tears
Weep my love
wash away the shadows
of yesterday's pain
let me hold you
while you die

Loving you

    is liquid sunlight

        on shimmering waters

I want to walk with you
                through the fields
                        naked to the sky
            our feet in the rich black earth
I want to feel the wind
                    on our nipples
            and the sun
                        between our legs
I want to look through you
                at the rippling wheat
                and blend your hair
                into the sweet clover

One day
      when it's time for me
            to die
     you will come into bed
              with me
      and gently
         I will leave

We climbed the canyon
                    dust in our eyes
each step gruelling
                    stones on the path
silence our companion
                    lips crying for water
pain in the air
                    blisters gnawing
seeking a ridge
                    our breath heavy
standing at last
                    together


                    so far apart

Now tell me truthfully
       is this love
              or isn't it
    I mean
        all this touching
        all this kissing
          and gazing
            and talking
              and sighing
          pales before
             the sacred
             the supernatural act
           of eating burned chicken
                      together

# Self-Floe

The prairie sky
        stretches my soul
   and leaves me no room
          to be small
  I connect with the infinite stars
      that draw me upwards
  out of my bony husk
    and spread me
       into distant galaxies

This moment of being awake
                    is a jewel
                              gleaming in the sunlight
          the clearness
                    the intensity
                            scares me
        it's like all my lights
                    are turned on
and I'm afraid of being blinded
        afraid
                if they stay on
                        I'll explode
      into a billion bits of light
             scattered through the universe
             never again coming together
and there is no more
                    me
        just particles
                  among the stars

Love
　　is the word
　　　　and I kiss the wet grass
　　　sweet dew
　　　　　　moistening my dry lips
　there is a cleanness in you
　　　　that empties me
　　　　　　　into your roots

I stand nourished
         by the black earth
                that roots me
    my ankles
        furrowed
             in sweet manure
      blended into my soles
          reaching to my brows
there is no feeling like it
there is no world
          but the earth
   brother to the cow
       sister to the horse
   standing where feet
            are meant to be
      standing
         rooted
             born to the moment

I want to fill up
          from within
     milk the nipples of my soul
     squeeze the tits of my being
I want to make love with
             the gods inside
     orgasm upon orgasm
   until death brings me around again
       full of white nectar
        and haloes of light

This is my birth moment
    the coming of my soul
        into humanity
    the God moment
      kissed by the angels
        delivered to my task
This is the moment of my earthing
      when I breathe my first
    and ask not to forget
      my holy guides
This is the moment of greeting
      my new keepers
    who shall harvest
      and sift me
        from the chaff
This is the moment
    when God and I
      smile at each other
    wish one another well
      and promise to write

I arrived like a prune
            creased
                        in no hidden spots
        withered
                        as a desert rock
        blasted
                    like an ancient stone
stuck between your legs
                    I writhed to be born
            counted near to death
                            and you too
                we separated
                            and gave each other
                                        life

I must sleep now
        in a different way
    sleep
       to know
           to understand
    sleep
       to pull the pearl
             from its bed
          and set it
             in a necklace of stars

I used to dream of a light
                    so strong
          I couldn't open my eyes
     when I tried
                    it hurt
          the whiteness was blinding
          like looking at the sun
     it seemed as if
                    there was something
                         I wasn't ready to see
     I'm not sure I'm ready now
          but I remember the dream
                    clearly
                              many times
          and feel it's time
               to begin seeing
                    behind the veil
          to peel away
                    my eyelids
               and not turn
                         my face

There is a crystal
      that reflects black light
   and in it
      I can see
        fragments of life
          from distant times
            and distant space
     it moves quickly
       affording only a glimpse
  except
      when it moves so quickly
         it stands still
    and all my lives
      are as one
     and I see myself
       as I am

What I like best
      about being alone
            is that I don't have to justify
                  my silence

I'm beginning to suspect
            I'm afraid of my power
     it's easier to be weak
          afraid of what might come out
                if I take off the lid
        easier to sleep
        and really scared
              to meet myself
                  in unfamiliar ways

I don't want to be a man
                    anymore
I'm tired of being too strong
                            to be nervous
            too strong
                        to be vulnerable
        taking it all in stride
                with a gun on each hip
    tired of being tough
                letting you know where things stand
                            in no uncertain terms
                being direct
                            like a shiv
    tired of having all the answers
            being afraid to admit
                    I don't understand the question
    tired of holding back my tears
            for fear they might stain
                            my image
            just
                tired
                    tired
                        tired
            of not being
                    human

Let my woman speak
    I who have lain dormant
        unable to puncture
                the fabric of male metal
        unable to push the heart seams
            from their narrow crevice
        now give voice
                to my longings
    I shall give you
        the softness of whispered love
        the tender feelings
            of a mother to her child
        the strength
            of understanding
        the endurance
            of labour
        the compassion
            of nursing
    I shall give you all this
            and more
    for without
        you are not yet
            a man

I didn't want to watch
        the slides of Poland tonight
    but the lights quickly went out
          after vanilla ice⁄cream
            chocolate syrup
            marshmallow topping
            whipped cream
            chopped nuts
                  & maraschino cherries
     the main course
            crematoriums
            numberless shoes without souls
            a room full of hair
            shower⁄heads that dripped gas
            bones and pieces of bones
            barracks
                row on row
                  lapping at the horizon
   In one way or another
        I've seen it all before
           again
              and
                again
  yet it's always new
        and the same questions nag at me
          with old answers
             that don't satisfy

I feel very alone

       and frightened

  at what is buried

         in my own heart

This jewish world
      flows past me
  I am of it
    and out of it
   weaving in and out
        of david's star
      not knowing my place
     then landing
         briefly
    re⁄rooted
  but always now
       briefly
   before moving on
        into galaxies
  where jew is not
  returning to solar dust
     our common mother

You hurt me
             badly
       when you kicked me
                      in the balls
             lifting your knee
                      like an anvil
             crushing me
                      in more ways
             than you could ever imagine
       locking rage
                      into my groin
             that remains
                      like bullets
                      on a frozen hair⁄trigger
and all because
                      I'm a Jew
             no other reason
one day
             should we ever meet again
                      I may kill you

I feel this skull
       inside my bones
   bleaching my life
         bringing me to
               ashes
    suddenly
        I feel old
      a million years have passed
           and still those sockets
          stare at me
        my soul winks back
            into the hollow orb
               of God's eye

I am clearly aware
        into the night

I am clearly aware
        past dreams
        past hollow fear
                through time⁄webs
                and labyrinth combs
      I fly
          soul⁄naked
              into the light
I am clearly aware
        and death observes me

I remember Jacob
            sitting by the tent
        silhouetted
                in the evening light
connected to the north sky
            drawing in the coloured dance
            charging his aura
                    with healing dust
    and the people came
                from the four winds
        touching him
                    with
                        hand
                    with
                            heart
                    with
                        tear
            and they left
                        less stooped
                        less creased
        lost fragments
                        restored
        lost hopes
                        rekindled
        lost tears
                        reclaimed

Sometimes
        I think I'm a toilet seat
            flipping up and down
                    all day
          carrying all kinds of weight
            and having to face
                a lot of dumping
        maybe it would be better
              to be the bowl
        and just take things
              as they come

I like the way my cock
            nestles softly into my balls
     like a bird
        feathering down
            upon her eggs

On this day of atonement              October 6, 1992
I atone
>   for all the pain
>> I have brought upon others
>   for all the pain
>> I have brought upon myself

I atone
>   for not listening
>> to my dreams
>   for not listening
>> to God

I atone
>   for changing channels
>> while I'm eating
>> so as not to see
>>> bones protuding
>>> from children's chests

I atone
>   for escaping into sleep
>> when staying awake
>>> might have made a difference

I atone
>   for fearing the pain
>> of an open heart
>   for loving less
>> when I could have loved more

I atone
>   for not lighting a candle
>> in the midst of darkness

I atone

Strange
      I feel very centred
          yet I'm hurting
     I always thought
            there would be no pain
         in my middle being
   It's like the pain of thawing
      when my feet unnumbed
        after hockey
   they were warming up
       but God it hurt
Now it's inside
        and the million pin⁄needles
       are undoing
    ice particles coming to the surface
    and the pain feels good

I feel like a sheet in the morning
   all wrinkled and full of creases
      and I want to be smoothed out
  all of me seen
     all of me felt
        all of me stretched
          all of me aired
  and then I want to be slept in again
            so I'm interesting

I want to laugh
        and crack the sky
    unclench my jaws
            and bellow to the stars
      there is a tumbling
              inside
       a rumbling
           of loose parts
        coming up
            to meet the day
     and I feel it all
       God
         I feel it all
      the ice is melting
      the dam is crumbling

# Root-Floe

I look into your eyes
          woman who nursed me
                    and gave me life
      soon now to leave
                 this place of breath
I try to unlock your thoughts
           steel encased
       meeting vacant looks
              and seldom words
    stroking your skin
           to touch your heart
still wanting your love
       however small the measure
still wanting your smile
       however cracked your lips
still wanting your hand
          to brush my hair

You sat by the large window
                not your usual place
          looking out at the sky
                  and the snow
          as if ready to step into them
There is no longer an age
                      on your face
          as if your soul
                  has come fully
                        into your eyes
              about to take leave
                    into the endless vision
                        of always
                            another tomorrow

You took a sip of water
                and died
         it was that simple

You told me about your pain today
      lovely man of my birth
      gentle soul in a twisted body
I want to kiss your wounds
         and draw your pain away
             into a distant pool
I want to take away
         every tear you have ever shed
         every anguish you have ever housed
    and brush your lids
           into a dream⁄filled sleep
              of cotton scenes
               and tulip hues

This gentle soul
       my father
hums on his pillow
              after a day of pain
      a lullaby
              his own
       to ease him into sleep
he touches me
              so deeply
I want to kiss him
              all over
and sing his child
       to a dream
              softly

My son
    I love you in ways I don't understand
        ways that are beautiful
                and painful
          tender
            and
               unspoken

I loved you from the first moment I saw you
    when you greeted me
             by opening your eyes
      and I said
         welcome son
    the purity of your soul
        that came to us that day
      has been undiminished
          through the years
    being near you
        and with you
            opens my heart
      and sometimes makes me afraid
      of the holiness I feel
         in your presence
    I thank God each day
        for your blessing

Son

    please stand up

           and yell at me

        when I yell at you

           and you feel angry

                  for being put down

      yell at me

          so I'll know

        some of your love for me

           hasn't been cut away

              by my tongue

My little girl
             now so grown
                          at not yet twelve
             when you come into my arms
                          without me asking
                                       in my many ways
             my heart leaps
                          and my soul is still
             I watch you listen
                          and know you hear
             I watch you connect
                          and see the bond
                  as I have seen your understanding
                          strong at a tender age
and I want more of that
                          that good stuff
             that you share so freely
                          with others
             I guess I'm a bit jealous
                          I need your love

Well sweetheart
      the reason I don't give you
               this bed
   to sleep on with your friend
   is because
      the sheets have just been changed for me
        I'm very tired
          it's late
   I have to get up early in the morning
      I have a busy day tomorrow
   besides
      what's wrong with where you're
               sleeping now
you waited patiently for me to finish my speech
Daddy why don't you just say you want to sleep here

# Life-Floe

Hanging out the trailer
     a magnificent
          horse's tail
  attached of course
     black to the moonless night
     glittering in the sun
       a thread of blue
    shimmering
          past the wind

sittin amongst
        you simple folk
   here in bluegrass country
      proteges of the unexamined life
         country-pickin folk
there's somethin clean
          and honest
     no pretenses
     no veneer
     no intellectual bullshit
an I'm settlin in
      to the good ol' times
    fiddlin with my ass
        on a hard bench
   an clappin the rhythm
      to a jauncy chord
     of a Mac Wiseman twang

Sloshin aroun
       in your beer
           bluegrass man
    kickin up the stones
         with a rata ta two
   belly⁄over⁄the⁄belt
           nothin to do
     'cept
        guzzle it down
            into your gut
            through your ears
       into some vestige
              of a soul
  bluegrass man
        watchagointado
     with the rest of your life
        kids n'wife n'all
      watchagointado
        bluegrass man
           watchagointado

Some work
            by the sweat of their brow
I work
        by the sweat of my balls
                    don't ask my why
                        don't ask me how
                    'cause I work hard
                        and I work now
                    and I don't care
                            if you know my way
                    I don't care
                        if you see my pay
                'cause I'm a man of now
                    a workin man
            yeh
                a workin man
            I'm a workin man
        comin around
                        one more time
                for a nickel
                            or a dime
            I'm a workin man
                            yeh

Each of us
            is locked away
                        in a mind cage
trying desperately to be free
                not knowing
    we can only open our eyes
                            so wide
            without becoming blind
            unless we first open them
                        in our dreams

Ultimately
        there is a very deep aloneness
                that sets in
        where neither God
                nor the angels
          dare intrude
      here is determined
          the quality of life
              to yet be lived
        and the quality of death
              to yet be known

we are all
        shovellers of dirt
sweepers
        under the carpet
watchers of the bulge
        as it grows
        concealed in pretty patterns
    that belie
        the underneath
we carpet our eyes
        and look away
    to one day find
we sit atop a mound
    of unexpected dimension
        and wonder
    where it all came from

He was a nice guy
       smiling politely
       speaking softly
       choosing the right word
       never a mean one to say
              about anybody
    never lifted his hand
            or raised his voice
            never protested
everyone had a kind word to say
            about him
      when his name came up
        now and then
       people smiled
      he knew how well he was thought of
      and when he died
      the inscription on his stone
         read
           at his request
     He Was A Nice Guy
     But Not Much Else

You were my first friend
              to teach me about
                          cruelty

                    and sex
        you didn't combine them
                    at least not to my knowledge
        but I remember you telling me
                    about some difficulty in getting it in
                                        sometimes
                    I wondered about that
                                putting it in
                    it all sounded so strange
                        but something inside me
                                    stirred

and then you sat one day
                    with a grasshopper
        methodically
                    with experience
                                and skill
                pulling off its legs
    I was fascinated
                    while something inside me
                                turned
        and then I had to hold back
                            my vomit
                    while you placed that legless creature
                            on the streetcar tracks
        still
            I went with you to look at it
                    after the streetcar passed by

I saw you come out of your room
      without a leg
        little girl
      hobbling on crutches
          as if they were toys
     and I stood still
         not daring to move
           lest I mock your amputation
   my heart
         leapt out of my body
           to caress your stump
       to take it in my hands
          and make it all better
       to grow for you
          another limb
       and see you whole
         dancing at your wedding
    with all this
        but a dim memory
      of something
          that never happened

Rubber baby
        I remember you taken from the jar
formaldehyde
            dripping from your mongolian eyes
you were so perfect
        I wanted to hold you
            and rock you
    tremoring
          I touched your skin
     almost afraid
          you might come alive
   wondering
      if a soul was trapped
          somewhere
        in this preserved flesh
   wondering
         where you might now be
    or if I might meet you
       as someone
          again

I don't know why I think about you today
           when I was so young
      we never met
                 and you were dead
                      Oh, so young
   a call in the night
                    and I went to pick you up
                    and I wrapped you in a sheet
                         with safety pins
                    as I held back the tears
        such a small form
                   and
                      frail
They never told me how you died
        and no one can ever tell me why
I picked you up in my arms
             and rolled you to a steel drawer
             and closed you inside
             and some of me with you
       it was so cold inside
            I went upstairs
                    washed my hands
        and wept into the night

I remember my child
    with no place to go
        so young
           and so dead
   looking for a reverence
     a sacred place
      and a sacred way
        to say goodbye
 there was no earth
     no air
       no water
    to ease the passage
so like Elisha
    I watched her ascend
       in a chariot of fire

Silvered Souls
    shimmering in the sunset glow
    wheelchairs
        waiting to release you
    into a land
        now longed for
    with pasture greener
          by far
      than the withered fields
      that no longer nourish your roots
Soon
    the next step of your journey
          begins
      not to be denied
      by any who take on flesh
        as their heritage
Soon
    into a wider dream
      you will awaken
    and know again
      the earth of your soul

# Soul-Floe

*This section could be sub-titled "Primary-Process-Poetry." As much as possible, I have tried to set my mind aside and let words, rhythms, feelings and intuitions flow from my core. Little regard has been paid to the words making sense, though at times they do. Many of the poems are probably best felt and not read.*

Pigeon your hole
    with a furry nut
  florescent green be damned
     watch the kernal
          unfold its rubber neck
        rolling off a broken roof
       not to be undone
    the cat's paw
        triggers multiple perches
    for scraggly feet
        and knickered toes

The time I had my last feelings memorized
              were happy times
                     popcorn times
              candy-floss memories
                     slipping down water slides
              somersault glitterings
                     on sparkling sands
              striped fragments
              as fresh in the moment
                     as yesterday
                            when they were born

I want to tickle you
                bickle you
        rumble and gesticule you
                unpretentiously
                        honeysuckle
                                try and true
                                        gikl you
                flamboyantly
                        trundle in your bundle
                and walk in your yok
                not to exclude
                        making you nude
                                imbued
                                somewhat vued
                                and very screwed

I am alone
      in the snow of summer
   no one cries
        for my soul
           in the night street
I am alone in my birth
         my death
            but a step away

Pigeon your hole
　　　　butterflies and butterballs
　　　　　　　　　　not withstanding
　　　　　　into a daliance of trinkets
　　　　　　　　where jellybeans dance
　　　　　　　　　　on polka-dot squares
　　　　　and candy-cane stripes
　　　　　　　　　　twirl their way
　　　　　to assorted heavens
　　　　　　　　　　of fluff-stuff
　　　　　and wondrous brittles
　　　　　of nutted mintops

The other place is an exit
            like going out of winter
      no intruder
                  walks on the grass
            flowering the open window
                  waiting for God
                        edgeless on a cliff
            so walk I now
                        beneath the coat of ice
                  and falter on the hearth
                              of tomorrow

I grew up to sing
            inside of you
     not knowing the flowers
            to bloom in the green

the june light
    shines through trees
        of curved leaves
            and white branches
    sparkling
      shedding a glow
         of candled warmth
       on nights
         of gentle dew
    softly
      on rainbow days
         it follows
           the heart of paths
       and in stillness
          moves the wind

This is let⁄go time
  casting the nuts of a bull
     into the ring
   swatting a fly
     as it comes in for a landing
        upside down
    parting my lips
      till my head disappears
  and eating
     sanded egg yolks
       in a pickle barrel
   not to mention
     seeds of a minisculated sigalopa
     rinds of circumcised bananas
     and the melted fringes
      of an unconventional
         icicle

There is nothing
        I would rather do
    than whittle a mind shaft
                    till it gleams
                        in yellow folds
                    of honeyed⁄cotton
            and pulls my soul
                        to impossible lengths
                of yes
                        and yes
                            and yes

Pull your consciousness
           down around your feet
      where its tentacles
        can suck into the earth
      enough of vision
             through the skull
        encumbered by illusion
           warped by ignorance
       a mist
         that vanishes
             with no trace
       think with your feet
          and walk the earth
        with dust
          on your lips

Skullmudge
        on pepper
     sprinkling my brain
      vespers of silt
           on leather straw
        nippling my lips
  all this and more
        raining
            through my pores
         skating on my veins
         sifting through my gut juice
    ahhhh
        I say
           ahhhh
              and double ahhhh
        scoot my jute

You are the

       white-fanged devil

          sheened in all your rapture

     not once delivering

          the unwanted acorn of truth

     yours is the hell of echoes

           not yet heard

      except in some distant

           cavern of the soul

          untried

                unwhipped

                    unscarred

breathe past

        the wisps of glossy candor

breathe past

        the scorn of hallowed rakes

   take into your breast

        the unfestered scallions

           of magic promises

   and bellow

         into the mist

           of timeless veils

         into the tunnels

           of forgotten hopes

I'm trying to make sense
        of things that don't make sense
    and it doesn't make sense
            to try and do this
somebody said to me the other day
        Jerry
            why don't you just be
        be what
            I said
        he smiled
                in his being way
        and somewhere inside
                swallowed an ego
        while I skipped after sunbeams
                and juggled bubbles
        squinting in the night
                around multiple orgasms
        and twiddling my toe
                at a moon⁄struck cow

Blood
      not bud
    but blood
I say
     blood and blood
   can you get blood
          from a dud
     not so
       but
       cud from a cow
          is how
      I take blood
         maybe yesterday
            maybe now

Frozen birds
        in a paper bag
            almost thawed
        melting in my hand
            as I draw each out
                    one by one
          and hold it gently
                 warmly
            watching it fly away
        wondering
            what parts of me
                    nestle in these feathers

Now is the time to tremble
        shake'n an' bake'n
                an' stake'n
      slough it all off
        rock⁄a⁄cock
              in a spindly tree⁄top
      shed'n the bed'n
          let Tide abide
               kidd'n aside
      dropp'n the scales
          worm'n and squirm'n
    bumpety bump
            on my rump
    look ma
        no hands